MEGHAN

MEGHAN

ROYAL DUCHESS AND MOTHER

Halima Sadat
Foreword by Brian Hoey

Contents

Foreword by Brian Hoey

Meghan's first year as Duchess of Sussex was an incredible one. A fairy-tale year in which she transformed herself seamlessly into being an enthusiastic and fully-fledged working member of the most famous family in the world. Becoming a princess and royal duchess at the same time, she is also allowed to use the feminine version of her husband's subsidiary titles if she wishes as the Countess of Dumbarton and Baroness Kilheel. But it wasn't as effortless as it may have appeared. Meghan has worked tremendously hard and applied herself with extreme dedication and determination, to become one of the most popular and admired of the younger generation of the Royal Family.

Meghan was married to Prince Harry, now the Duke of Sussex, in a spectacular wedding at the historic 15th-century St George's Chapel in Windsor Castle in May 2018. It was attended by The Queen, the Duke of Edinburgh and every senior member of the Royal Family. It was also watched by millions throughout the world. One of the most endearing sights during the ceremony was when Meghan's new father-in-law, Prince Charles, offered his arm to her mother, Doria, as they processed down the aisle at St George's after Harry and Meghan had been pronounced man and wife.

As the first woman of mixed-race heritage to have reached into the very heart of Britain's first family – and been welcomed by them all – the Duchess of Sussex has already carved a unique place in history. The Prince of Wales has expressed his admiration and affection for her many times, and their relationship is developing into a close and loving bond. Meghan has said that Charles has been a 'pillar of strength' since the time they have known each other and his support grows with each passing day.

She is already devoting herself to her royal duties and charities, carrying on as she began – as a humanitarian and feminist – and continuing the outstanding contribution she made as a representative of the United Nations in the promotion of gender equality. She was thrown in at the deep end shortly after the wedding when she accompanied Prince Harry (to most people he is still known by this name even after being created Duke of Sussex by The Queen) on a strenuous tour that included Australia, New Zealand, Fiji and Tonga. It was an outstanding success with Meghan proving that she was quite capable of withstanding the rigours of royal duties and the non-stop attention of the media, whose voracious appetite focused on everything she ate, drank, wore, used and said. Meghan has a reserve of inner strength that enables her to be steadfast in all conditions, and as an experienced and established actress in the successful television series *Suits*, that was seen in many countries, she knows how to conduct herself in every situation.

Already Meghan is being compared to other ladies who have married into royalty, particularly her husband's mother, the late Diana, Princess of Wales, who, like Meghan, rapidly became the most photographed woman in the world.

Meghan, too, has become a fashion icon for young women throughout the world with copies of every outfit she wears selling out in days. It has been a roller-coaster year in many ways: her second Christmas with The Queen at Sandringham, this time as a full member of the Royal Family; the announcement of her expected baby in the spring of 2019; planning the move from Nottingham Cottage at Kensington Palace to the Grade II listed Frogmore Cottage within the grounds of the Home Park on the Windsor Castle Estate; and, of course, the birth of her first child.

To add to the excitement of Meghan's first year as Duchess of Sussex, The Queen handed over two of her own royal patronages to her new granddaughter-in-law and she became patron of the Royal National Theatre and the Association of Commonwealth Universities. It was a personal vote of confidence from Her Majesty. With Meghan's background in the acting profession and interest in education, they are surely subjects very close to her heart. These are just two of many patronages to which she will devote close attention in the years to come, with others following as she assumes an increasing number of public duties.

So, all in all a wonderful year that has seen this beautiful young American burst onto the British scene with an elegance and grace that has added a sprinkling of Hollywood glamour to the traditional qualities expected of royalty. And now, with Harry and Meghan as new parents, what joy the years ahead will bring.

California Girl

In the space of just a few months, Rachel Meghan Markle, known as Meghan, became one of the most famous women in the world. When she entered the British Royal Family following her marriage to Prince Harry, and, indeed, in the months preceding it, her face was splashed across the media all over the world, but who exactly was this woman who had suddenly become a household name?

Born in Los Angeles on 4 August 1981, Meghan is a true California girl who grew up in the suburbs of LA. It is a place where dreams really can come true, although it is almost certain that Meghan could never have expected to one day meet her real-life prince and have her life transformed so dramatically.

The daughter of award-winning lighting director Thomas Markle, of English, Irish and Dutch descent, and Doria Ragland, an African-American yoga teacher, social worker and psychotherapist, Meghan lived in the leafy suburb of Woodland Hills, an affluent area lying in the San Fernando Valley, not far from the Santa Monica Mountains. Although comfortable, her parents could not have been described as wealthy, unlike some of the other local residents, yet the family enjoyed the relaxed way of life and the excellent facilities the area has to offer.

It had not always been so for Meghan's parents, however, and it was a world away from the lives of their antecedents. On her father's side, Meghan's family were coal miners who had moved to the USA from Yorkshire

ABOVE: An aerial view of the LA suburbs where Meghan grew up

OPPOSITE: The iconic Hollywood sign in the Hollywood Hills

in England in 1859, in search of a new life. The Markles settled in Mahanoy City in the Appalachians, where they continued with the work to which they were accustomed, and it was there that Meghan's father was born in 1945.

As in so many mining areas, the young men sought lives away from the hard work underground and Thomas was no exception. Soon after leaving school he moved to Chicago and became a stage technician in theatre and television. Eventually, the bright lights of Hollywood beckoned and he enjoyed considerable success in his chosen career, winning a Daytime Emmy for Outstanding Achievement in Design Excellence for his work on the soap opera *General Hospital*. Although he worked in a glamorous industry, Thomas remained a quiet, private man; now retired, he lives in Mexico, in a house overlooking the Pacific Ocean.

Thomas was initially married to Roslyn Loveless with whom he had two children, Thomas Junior and Samantha. However, the marriage failed and several years passed before he met and married Doria Ragland.

Doria can trace her ancestry back to the Deep South and the slavery that was once widespread in that area. Meghan's grandfather, Alvin, married twice and Doria, born in Cleveland, Ohio in 1956, was the product of his first marriage to Jeanette Johnson. Not long after Doria's birth, the couple moved to Los Angeles, where Alvin opened his own bric-a-brac and antiques store.

Doria grew up and started working as a make-up artist; when training she worked on the set of *General Hospital* in the late 1970s, alongside Thomas Markle, the show's lighting director. Now divorced from Roslyn, he and Doria got to know each other and discovered a shared interest in antiques. They married in 1979 and Meghan was born two years later.

Sadly, the marriage was not to last. When Meghan was six they divorced, with Doria retaining custody of her. Fortunately, her parents' split was amicable and, through his weekend custody of her, Meghan maintained a good relationship with her father. Nevertheless, she was particularly close to her mother, who encouraged her to take pride in her African-American heritage and to become the woman she wanted to be. Doria was, and remains, a powerful role model to her daughter.

Doria had always been interested in helping those less fortunate and took Meghan to countries such as Jamaica and Mexico to visit impoverished communities, aiming to show Meghan that not everyone had the privileges she enjoyed.

Meghan was privately educated, attending the Hollywood Little Red Schoolhouse until she was 11. The school offered a mix of traditional core subjects, as well as topics tailored to each child's specific interests. Taking part in school plays and music performances formed an important part of the school's curriculum.

From there, in 1992, despite her Protestant background, Meghan moved to the all-girl Roman Catholic Immaculate Heart High School, where she was a diligent and popular student, elected Homecoming Queen for her 1998 school prom. Meanwhile, her interest in drama had continued and she found that Immaculate Heart offered more acting opportunities in a variety of roles, covering drama, musical theatre and comedy.

Fox Studios, where Meghan's father worked

During this time Meghan spent many hours after school in the Fox television recording studios with her father. She witnessed first-hand not only the mechanics of television acting but also the effort her father put into his work. She realised that the only way to achieve one's goals is to strive for them, an ethos that stayed with her as she grew up.

With the seeds that made Meghan consider a career as an actress already sown, she was ever-more convinced this was the route she wanted to follow. Knowing such a career could be precarious and highly competitive, she wisely decided to gain alternative qualifications should her aim prove unsuccessful. On leaving school, she attended the Northwestern University School of Communication, near Chicago, majoring in theatre and international studies and graduating in 2003.

It was during her studies that she undertook an internship that was to stand her in good stead in the future. She travelled to Argentina to work in the US embassy in Buenos Aires where, in addition to learning to speak Spanish, she gained a valuable insight into the world of diplomacy and the workings of government policy.

Hollywood Star

Following her experiences acting on stage at school and attending the Fox recording studios with her father, Meghan had set her heart on becoming an actress. When she eventually left university, her view had not changed. However, despite having grown up a stone's throw from the famous Hollywood sign and having a father in the business, the path to fame and fortune was not going to be as easy as she might have hoped. First, there was the competition, with hundreds of other hopeful young women all trying to follow their dream; second, because of her mixed-race background, Meghan often felt at a disadvantage. When going to auditions she always seemed to be too dark for white parts and too light for black parts.

As a result, the parts did not fall into her lap and, like many aspiring actresses, she had to fall back on other work to make ends meet. In Meghan's case, as a way of supplementing her income from the few bit parts and modelling jobs that came her way, she was able to call upon a skill she had acquired at Immaculate Heart, that of calligraphy. Her school had placed high value on neat handwriting, even requiring students to attend classes, and Meghan was able to make use of this ability as her 'pseudo waitress work' as she liked to call it, designing items such as invitations and handwritten correspondence, frequently for celebrity clients.

Early acting parts were small, with her first credit coming in 2002 for delivering a few lines as Nurse Jill in the soap *General Hospital*, the set on which her parents had originally met. In 2004 she appeared in *Century City*, a sci-fi legal drama that

ABOVE: Meghan Markle attends TV Guide Magazine's 2012 Hot List party in Hollywood

OPPOSITE: Meghan Markle in 2014, at an Elton John AIDS Foundation event in New York

Meghan arrives for the world premiere of *The Hunger Games: Catching Fire* in Leicester Square, London in 2013

only aired five shows, and this was followed in 2005 by a small part in the film *A Lot Like Love*.

Despite any difficulties she faced, Meghan was determined not to give up and in 2006 won a guest-star role in *The War at Home*, and later that same year in *CSI: NY*, followed by her first TV movie, *Deceit*.

Meghan was acquiring more screen exposure and in 2007 became something of a familiar face during primetime family viewing as the holder of suitcase number 24 on the popular game show *Deal or No Deal*. This show required Meghan to wear a short dress and negotiate the studio staircase in vertiginous heels – cheap shoes that she later admitted made her feet sore. She had to keep a fixed smile on her face and, whenever a contestant chose her suitcase, to appear thrilled or disappointed when the contents were revealed.

Vicky Huang, Meghan Markle and Chelsey Reist in the 2014 TV film *When Sparks Fly*

The years 2008 and 2009 saw small roles in the television shows *90210*, *Knight Rider*, *Without a Trace* and *The League*, and in 2010 she appeared in *CSI: Miami*. During this period she also began to win roles in full-length films, such as *Remember Me* starring Robert Pattinson and Pierce Brosnan, *Get Him to the Greek*, starring Russell Brand (although she had no lines and no credit), and, in 2011, *Horrible Bosses*, with Jennifer Aniston and Colin Farrell. These mainstream, high-grossing films represented Meghan's break into the big screen, but it was still tough to make a good living. Not only were parts hard to come by but there was also the on-set behind-the-scenes backbiting to deal with and the ignominy of having scenes ending up on the cutting room floor. While putting on the deceptive appearance of a thick skin, Meghan was demoralised, but she was still not about to give up on her dream. She was determined to succeed at her chosen profession, despite the setbacks, and that success came in 2010, when she won a role that she was to make her own.

> success came in 2010, when she won a role that she was to make her own

Having chased the Hollywood dream, ironically it was away from that hub of the film industry that Meghan finally made her name as an actress. For this, she had to travel north to Toronto in Canada – a city that was to become her adopted home – where she played the part she became best known for: Rachel Zane, in the legal drama series *Suits*, made by the cable network USA.

The studio had found the part difficult to cast, calling for someone unique to play the smart, elegant, well-educated paralegal with sex appeal; someone who could portray the character's confidence, yet combine it with a sense of vulnerability; someone who could appeal to viewers and create a connection with them.

The pilot for the show was screened in June 2011 and it was deemed a success. The show's popularity continued to grow and with it Meghan's acting career. She was fast becoming a household name, having been thrown into the spotlight in North America as viewing figures increased. Before long a fan base developed and further series of the show were planned.

Interestingly, Rachel Zane's bi-racial heritage was the topic of much discussion among the show's fans, some delighted to see an African-American portrayed in a

Meghan Markle with fellow *Suits* star Gina Torres in 2012 during the 'A More Perfect Union: Stories of Prejudice and Power' event in California, part of a campaign to combat prejudice and discrimination

positive light, others criticising that Meghan wasn't black enough. As for Meghan, she saw the role as her opportunity to demonstrate that it is possible for black women to break through the glass ceiling of gender and racial discrimination to become successful in their chosen field. This determination to achieve was further emphasised by Rachel Zane's struggle to pass her exams to enable her to become a fully qualified lawyer, perhaps a reflection of Meghan's own bumpy career path that had finally led her to success as a recognised actress.

Sarah Rafferty, Rick Hoffman, Meghan Markle and Patrick J. Adams at the NBC Universal Press Tour All Star Party in Los Angeles in 2011

Meghan (far left) with other stars from the TV drama *Suits* in 2013

Meanwhile, in September 2011, Meghan had married her long-term boyfriend, film producer Trevor Engelson. The couple had started dating in 2004, having met through their work. However, their heavy workloads and long periods spent apart led to divorce in August 2013.

By the end of 2013, *Suits* was the American television show with the highest ratings among the age group 18–45. Meghan suddenly found herself considered 'hot property', with plenty of invitations to red-carpet events and a salary to match her status. Walking the red carpet was not something she enjoyed, however, admitting it made her 'nervy and itchy'; rather, it was the acting and the opportunity to work with interesting people that attracted her to the film world. It was not the accompanying fame that she craved; recognition as a successful and competent actress was her priority.

There was an added bonus arising from her *Suits* fame. Now that she had made a name for herself, during the breaks from filming the series Meghan started to find it much easier to win other roles. Nevertheless, she also experienced a negative side to appearing in a popular television show and received aggressive messages from fans who were unable to dissociate real life from fantasy: they disapproved of Rachel cheating on Mike Ross by kissing her previous boyfriend. Alarmed at the way the script was heading and the change in Rachel's characterisation, Meghan was able to convince the show's producer to retain Rachel's likeability, evidence of both her ability to influence others and her strong sense of integrity.

In total, Meghan appeared in seven series of *Suits*, seeing her character progress from being a young paralegal to becoming a confident fully-fledged attorney. By the end of the seventh series, which came to a close in April 2018, Meghan had met her real-life future husband, Prince Harry, and she was to walk down the aisle twice in the space of a few weeks, when, as a poetic close to her time in the show, Rachel Zane's last appearance was as a bride, marrying Mike Ross.

Meghan's time in *Suits* was over and, much to the dismay of her fans, so was her career as an actress. Having accepted that this era was to end for her, she looked forward with enthusiasm to the next stage of her life, when she would not only be the wife of a senior member of the British Royal Family, but she would also be able to devote more time to her second passion, that of helping to improve the lives of those less fortunate.

ABOVE: Rachel Zane (Meghan Markle) with Mike Ross (Patrick J. Adams) in *Suits*, 2016
OPPOSITE: Meghan Markle as her *Suits* character Rachel Zane in 2017

A Passion for Change

One of the character traits that has drawn the public to Meghan is her passion for issues that she cares deeply about. This, along with her warm personality and caring nature, has won her a place in the nation's heart, as well as that of her husband, who has said that he was initially attracted to her because of their shared interests and, in some ways, the similar experiences of their early lives. In Harry's case, his mother Diana was keen to show her sons that there was another side to life, away from the privileged trappings of being princes. She took the boys to homeless shelters and to visit AIDS victims to help them understand the difficulties some people face, two issues that she felt particularly strongly about.

OPPOSITE: Meghan Markle on her visit to Rwanda in 2016

Meghan, too, far away in California, was growing up in affluent surroundings, and, like Diana, her mother Doria also wanted to show her daughter that there are many others less fortunate. The plight of impoverished people, powerless to improve their lot, had a huge effect on Meghan and the desire to do something to help those without a voice has remained one of her priorities.

Childhood experiences affected her in other ways too. Growing up she was aware that she was bi-racial, but it wasn't until she experienced racism directed at her mother that she realised the extent of both the racial discrimination and racial stereotyping prevalent in America. She was horrified to discover that, because of her pale complexion, she was often assumed to be her mother's charge rather than her daughter, her mother taken for the nanny and not the parent. She was even more alarmed when, on one occasion in particular, she witnessed her mother being verbally abused in a racist fashion by a driver displaying road rage. As a result of these early experiences and, later, her problems at castings due to her mixed heritage, racial equality was to become another area upon which she focused her attention.

Meghan was not destined to become an extreme activist at demonstrations, rather she chose the route of quiet influence, making her case calmly and logically to organisations and individuals with the power to bring about change. The first evidence of her ability to get others to pay attention to what she had to say came in 1993 when she was just 11 and incensed by an advertisement on television for Ivory washing up liquid that contained the words 'women all over America are fighting greasy pots and pans'. Her anger was exacerbated when two male classmates, during the ensuing discussion in a social science lesson focused on advertisements, proclaimed that women 'belong' in the kitchen.

While she might not have labelled herself a feminist at that point in her life, Meghan was outraged and determined to have her say. She wrote a letter explaining her objection to the advert's wording, not only to Proctor & Gamble, the manufacturers of the product in question, but also to civil rights lawyer Gloria Allred and Linda Ellerbee, host of children's television channel Nickelodeon's *Nick News*. Finally, she wrote to the then First Lady Hillary Clinton.

Megan Markle and other celebrities visiting the US Army base Sigholtz Center, Italy in 2014

Her efforts brought results as soon afterwards Proctor & Gamble amended the wording in the advert to say 'people' instead of 'women', just as she had suggested in her letter, and Meghan featured on *Nick News* speaking about her success. In her quiet, unassuming yet positive voice, the young girl from California had some words of advice for other children, telling them that if there was anything they saw on television or elsewhere that offended them they should 'write letters and send them to the right people', adding, 'you can really make a difference not only for yourself but for a lot of other people'. Meghan realised that she really did have a voice, and she could use it to implement change for the better.

Since then, Meghan has continued to be interested in gender equality. As an adult working in the film industry, which is still male dominated today, she was acutely aware of how difficult it was for her to get ahead as a woman and that she was often defined by her physical attractiveness rather than for her acting ability. Even on the set of *Suits*, she felt she had to strike a blow for feminism when yet another script required her to appear fresh from the shower in a towel. It was once too often; Meghan put her foot down, refusing to do what she saw as a gratuitous pandering to the male audience.

Speaking about this, she has said that she felt empowered by her decision and that she believes strongly that women must not only be heard, they must also be listened to. It was this attitude, following a blog that she had written on personal independence to tie in with Independence Day, that led to her being invited by the Senior Adviser to the Executive Director of UN Women to work as an advocate to help promote women's rights.

Meghan was keen to accept, but she felt ill-prepared for the task, knowing little about the United Nation's work and how the organisation functioned. To better equip herself, she requested to be allowed to shadow employees at the UN headquarters in New York. As an actress, she found she had no suitable office attire, but after borrowing a few outfits belonging to her *Suits* character Rachel, she set off for the city to immerse herself in the UN culture, attending briefings with the UN Secretary General's team and seeing for herself the work being undertaken by the UN on a daily basis.

Before long, in January 2016, she was offered the opportunity to travel to Rwanda, to find out more about the education of girls and their aspirations in a country that, after being torn apart by civil war in the 1990s, was finally recovering from its effects. What especially interested Meghan was the fact that, at the time of her visit, Rwanda was the country, out of all others in the world, to have the highest percentage of women in parliament; she was curious to discover how women had empowered themselves to achieve this remarkable state of affairs. She took time to talk to women of all ages, and also visited a refugee camp that was home to 17,000

> she was offered the opportunity to travel to Rwanda

people who had fled the civil war raging in the Democratic Republic of Congo. She later wrote about her experience, 'This type of work is what feeds my soul.' Her time in Rwanda gave her an insight into a world seemingly light years away from her life back home. In 2016, she became a World Vision Global Ambassador to help bring clean water to parts of Rwanda that until then still had no proper water supply.

Meghan in Rwanda; she was delighted to be able to work with World Vision to help provide access to clean water in rural areas of the country

On her return from Rwanda, she resumed her acting roles, but also continued with her UN Women work. She attended meetings at the World Bank and the Clinton Foundation to hear about gender bias in the West and later that year delivered a speech as the UN Women's Advocate for Women's Leadership and Political Participation. The event was to mark the 20th anniversary of the Fourth World Conference of Women in Beijing and, nervously, Meghan spoke in front of the great and the good from the UN and other leading world organisations.

Her nerves were soon dissipated as she recalled her action from years earlier as an 11-year-old, summing up her views on gender equality with these profound words, 'Women need a seat at the table … and where this isn't available, they need to create their own table. It isn't enough to simply talk about equality, one must believe in it and it isn't enough to simply believe in it, one must work at it.'

Meghan speaking at the UN Women event 'Step It Up For Gender Equality' in 2015

Meghan had already shown, and was continuing to show, that she could follow and demonstrate her own philosophy.

On her engagement to Harry in 2017, Meghan had to relinquish her associations with some of her favoured charities and campaigns to work more closely with her fiancé. Harry has introduced some new charitable areas to Meghan, such as those related to mental health, disability sport and injured servicemen; however, many of their interests have also aligned, in particular issues relating to Africa and the plight of people in disadvantaged communities – especially in relation to children and young people – and conservation. This is the work that she carries out with Harry, her brother-in-law William and his wife Catherine through the Royal Foundation, which is described as the 'primary philanthropic and charitable vehicle for the Duke and Duchess of Cambridge and the Duke and Duchess of Sussex'.

Prince Harry, Meghan Markle and the Duchess and Duke of Cambridge at the first Royal Foundation Forum; the theme 'Making a difference together' showcased programmes initiated by the Foundation

Originally started by William and Harry in 2009, their wives have joined the Royal Foundation following marriage. Even prior to her wedding, Meghan showed that she was going to be a forthright and valuable asset. Her commitment was evident when she spoke eloquently at the Royal Foundation Forum in February 2018, explaining that she was ready 'to hit the ground running' and that she was intending to 'maximise the opportunity we have here to really make an impact'.

> a Foundation that ... will truly build positive change

Dubbed the 'Fab Four', together they have created a Foundation that, through the influence and power that both couples can bring to bear, will truly build positive change and help countless individuals and communities face a brighter future.

Meghan meets panellists and beneficiaries at the Royal Foundation Forum in London, February 2018

A Royal Romance

Mystery surrounds the identity of the mutual female friend who introduced Meghan to Harry by setting them up on a blind date, having detected that these two dynamic people would get along famously. It was May 2016 and Harry happened to be in Toronto, the city in which Meghan was living, to launch the countdown to the Invictus Games to be held there in 2017. This mutual friend decided it was the perfect opportunity to indulge in a little matchmaking.

Having informed Harry that she had an attractive friend whom he should meet, the person in question set about persuading Meghan that she might have an enjoyable time in Prince Harry's company. Meghan knew nothing about Harry or

OPPOSITE: Prince Harry and Meghan Markle on the day their engagement was announced

the British Royal Family, so was uncertain. Before committing herself, Meghan's question to her friend was simple and straightforward: 'Is he nice?' Having been assured that indeed he was, she agreed to meet him.

As Harry walked into the venue selected for their meeting, he spotted the stunning Meghan waiting for him. Just as Meghan had little prior knowledge of Harry, he was unfamiliar with her as an actress, having never seen the programme *Suits*. As a result, the pair met with no preconceptions or expectations, which meant they could relax immediately and be at ease together.

For Harry, this was especially significant as his status as one of the world's most eligible bachelors had the potential to overawe any woman. In fact, Meghan was more impressed by this good-looking English gentleman with a sense of humour than by his status, while Harry has admitted to being smitten with Meghan at first sight.

> Harry has admitted to being smitten with Meghan at first sight

Conversation flowed easily and Harry and Meghan found that they had a great deal in common – for example, their shared love of Africa and, most importantly, their mutual desire to do something meaningful with their lives to help others less fortunate, especially in countries with high levels of deprivation and poverty.

So keen were they to meet for a second time that a date was arranged for the following day. Harry was completely bowled over by this beautiful and intelligent woman who had suddenly and unexpectedly entered his life. It just so happened that he had a trip to Botswana planned, due to take place a few weeks later. He was to go there as a member of an elephant translocation project and decided to ask Meghan to join him there for a few days' holiday so that they could get to know each other a little better. As they had only had two dates, Harry considered his suggestion to be a 'huge leap', but he took a chance and was more than delighted when Meghan accepted.

In the quiet seclusion of the African bush the couple were able to relax, away from the glare of publicity and the pressures of their day-to-day lives. For Harry,

ABOVE: Prince Harry with Canadian Prime Minister Justin Trudeau, Toronto Mayor John Tory and sledge hockey athletes in Toronto, May 2016; during his visit to the city he was introduced to Meghan Markle

LEFT: Meghan Markle at a Hollywood party in May 2016, the month she first met Prince Harry

Africa has always been a very special place where he is free to be himself and feels, in his words, 'plugged into the earth'. As he enthusiastically shared the smells, sights and sounds of Botswana, he was delighted to find that Meghan too had a special affection for that continent, having been involved in the not-too-distant past in the World Vision project in Rwanda.

Sharing a tent in 'the middle of nowhere', far from the comforts of modern life, Harry could see that Meghan was a woman who embraced a challenge and was in touch with the world around her. Together they enjoyed watching the spectacle of the luminous African stars travelling across the night sky, the stars that Harry went on to say were 'aligned' to create the love that was starting to grow between them.

All too soon the short holiday was over and it was back to reality – Harry returning to London and Meghan to Toronto to continue with her acting career. Both were keen for their relationship to develop further, but Harry, remembering the problems that his mother had experienced, was all too aware of the pressures that could be brought to bear if news of it became public knowledge too soon. He felt that if he and Meghan were to have a chance together, then their romance would have to be conducted in secret.

Consequently, there were to be no dates to restaurants, parties or functions, but, instead, quiet evenings at home with just the two of them or the company of a few trusted friends. The tricky situation was further exacerbated by their living on opposite sides of the Atlantic; but despite frequent trips back and forth between the UK and Canada, no suspicions were aroused.

Of course, this situation couldn't continue indefinitely and eventually news leaked out that Harry had a serious girlfriend. The media went into overdrive: Meghan found herself under an unwelcome and critical spotlight, her every move monitored and reported. Much was made of her African-American heritage and, in some quarters, it was suggested that this alone was a barrier to her ever being accepted as a member of the Royal Family.

As the level of sexist and racist criticism increased, Harry took the unusual step for a member of the Royal Family of issuing a formal personal statement demanding that Meghan's detractors treat her with dignity and respect, stating that 'this is not a game, it is her life'. He was not going to allow the media to destroy his relationship and, most importantly, he was not prepared for Meghan to suffer at the hands of the media in the way his mother had done so many years earlier.

Many women would have been alarmed by this unwelcome press intrusion, but Meghan had the maturity and strength of character to deal with the criticism and pressure that she found herself subjected to. Her feelings for Harry were strong and she was not prepared for their love to fall at the first hurdle.

The relationship might have been out in the open, but Meghan and Harry continued to keep a low profile, and outings where they might be seen together were limited. It was not until September 2017 that the pair appeared in public and made it clear that they were a strong, united couple. The occasion was the Invictus Games, a major sporting event for injured servicemen and women, that were being held in Meghan's then home town of Toronto. Having been set up originally by Harry in 2014, it is perhaps not surprising that it was at the Games that he chose to publicly show off his girlfriend and, in so doing, make a formal statement of their

LEFT: Officially a couple, Meghan and Harry are photographed holding hands at the Invictus Games, September 2017

BELOW: Prince Harry and Meghan Markle stand next to their good friend Markus Anderson, seen hugging Meghan's mother Doria Ragland, at the closing ceremony for the 2017 Invictus Games; on the far left is another of Meghan's friends, Canadian fashion stylist Jessica Mulroney

feelings for one another. Although they sat apart at the opening ceremony, it wasn't long before they were seen together watching the wheelchair tennis tournament, and then, to the delight of the crowds, strolling around the venue hand in hand, relaxed and happy in each other's company.

After four days of sport, the final evening of the Games arrived, when Meghan was able to witness Harry's passion and commitment to the event as he delivered his moving speech prior to the closing ceremony. As the Invictus Games closed, Harry joined Meghan and her mother in the Air Canada suite. The chemistry between the young couple and the easy relationship Harry had with Doria was noted by onlookers, the picture finally being completed by Harry kissing his girlfriend. Whereas the press had previously been talking of a relationship, the couple's romantic interaction turned the media's attention quickly towards news of a potential engagement.

That engagement came just two months later when, on 27 November 2017 at 10am, the official announcement that His Royal Highness Prince Henry of Wales and Ms Meghan Markle were to marry was issued by Clarence House. By this time, Meghan had left *Suits* and had moved into Harry's two-bedroom house, Nottingham Cottage, in the grounds of Kensington Palace. It was there that, much to Meghan's surprise, the proposal took place, while the couple were cooking roast chicken. In contrast to many modern proposals, Harry's was without flamboyance, which Meghan later described as 'so sweet, so natural and very romantic'.

Just days after the announcement Meghan accompanied her fiancé on her first official public appearance when the couple visited Nottingham to attend a charity fair marking World AIDS day. The event was particularly poignant as Harry pledged that, with Meghan at his side, he would carry on his mother's work campaigning for AIDS awareness. For Meghan, with hundreds of well-wishers lining the city's streets, it was her first taste of the adulation of 'Meghan fever'. If she had had any apprehension about the event it was not apparent; she is a natural when it comes to relating to others of all ages from all walks of life and talked with ease to the local people.

The date for the wedding was set, but before then Meghan found herself introduced not only to the rest of Harry's family but also to the UK as a whole, with

ABOVE: Meghan's engagement ring features a large central diamond sourced from Botswana; this is flanked by two smaller diamonds, once part of the jewellery collection belonging to Princess Diana

RIGHT: Harry and Meghan greet the press following their engagement on 27 November 2017

OPPOSITE (ABOVE): Harry and Meghan are greeted by well-wishers during a visit to Cardiff Castle, January 2018

OPPOSITE (BELOW): Just a few weeks after Meghan and Harry were engaged, they follow The Queen, Prince Philip and the Duke and Duchess of Cornwall as they leave St Mary Magdalene Church in Sandringham, Norfolk, on Christmas Day 2017

further official visits to Scotland, Northern Ireland and Wales. At each location the couple visited local enterprises. In Edinburgh it was to Social Bite, a restaurant that supports the homeless; in Belfast they toured Titanic Belfast, a tourist attraction that charts Belfast's maritime history, as well as the city dockyards; and in Wales they enjoyed a celebration of Welsh culture at Cardiff Castle, along with a demonstration of the activities that take place at the STAR Hub leisure centre which offers sporting opportunities for disadvantaged youngsters.

In addition, the pair took a trip nearer to home when they went to Brixton in south London, where they proved extremely popular at local community radio station Reprezent, which works hard to reduce knife crime, while helping young people to develop socially and acquire skills for employment in the media.

Meghan's African-American heritage was of huge significance to the residents of this largely black area, thereby adding a new nuance to her relationship with the British public.

It was only to be a few months before Meghan became a formal member of the Royal Family, but in the run-up to the wedding it was clear that she had earned respect and admiration within the Royal Family itself and beyond. Indeed, normal protocol was abandoned when Meghan – not yet married to Harry – was invited to enjoy a traditional royal Christmas at Sandringham in Norfolk, where all members of the family gather every year as guests of The Queen.

Wedding Bells

On 19 May 2018, Windsor dawned fine and warm, a beautiful spring day. Among the crowds who were gathering in anticipation of the day's events, some of whom had camped out overnight to secure the perfect vantage point, there ran an almost tangible ripple of excitement. Those in the town the previous evening had enjoyed an impromptu walkabout by the groom and his best man, Harry's brother William; now they waited for a glimpse of the bride as she travelled to St George's Chapel within the grounds of Windsor Castle, where the ceremony was due to take place.

Prior to her arrival, the brothers had walked to the chapel to take their places at the front of the church. Also arriving were 600 guests – many from the world of

ABOVE: The groom and his best man wait for the bride to arrive

OPPOSITE: Harry and Meghan share a kiss as they leave St George's Chapel after their wedding ceremony

acting, music and sport – attired in designer outfits, complete with the most splendid hats, as stipulated by the wedding dress code.

Members of the Royal Family also walked to the church and, in keeping with tradition, The Queen and Prince Philip were last to arrive. Watching this remarkable procession, and first to see the bride as she stepped out of the 1950s Rolls-Royce Phantom IV, were around 1,500 members of the public who had been invited into the confines of Windsor Castle. These comprised a mix of charity workers, local schoolchildren, members of the Royal Household and Crown Estate, and community members of Windsor Castle itself.

Unfortunately, Meghan's father Thomas was unable to attend the marriage due to ill health, while another absent family member was Prince Louis, the youngest son of Prince William and his wife Catherine. At three weeks old, he was deemed a little too young to participate in the day.

As meticulously planned, at 11.59am precisely the Rolls-Royce conveying Meghan and her mother arrived at the steps of St George's Chapel, to the accompaniment of a specially composed fanfare by the State Trumpeters. As Meghan exited the car, her stunning gown was revealed for the first time.

A simple design from French fashion house Givenchy, the boat-neck, waisted gown with a full skirt was made from double-bonded silk cady with an underskirt of triple silk organza. The dress also held a small secret: sewn into it, hidden from view, was a discreet piece of fabric from the blue dress that Meghan had worn on

Meghan arrives at St George's Chapel

her first date with Harry – a romantic gesture that satisfied the 'something blue' tradition that promises good luck for a new bride. The dress represented elegant, modern and pared-down chic, created through soft tailoring and impeccable cut. It was complemented by an ornate 16-foot (five-metre), lace-edged silk tulle veil embroidered with floral emblems from the 53 Commonwealth countries, as well as wintersweet, which grows in the garden of Nottingham Cottage, and the California poppy, the official flower of Meghan's home state.

With her hair in a soft chignon, Meghan's veil was held in place by a beautiful platinum tiara, heavily decorated with diamonds and featuring a central detachable brooch, itself containing ten diamonds. The tiara, originally given to Queen Mary on her marriage in 1893 to the then Prince George, Duke of York, was lent to Meghan by The Queen; to complement it, Meghan wore a pair of simple diamond earrings and a bracelet by Cartier.

To tie in with the theme of her dress, Meghan carried an understated yet elegant bouquet containing blooms specially selected by Prince Harry himself and handpicked from the couple's private garden in Kensington Palace. Also in the

Meghan walks down the aisle followed by her four pageboys and six bridesmaids, amongst them Prince Harry's nephew and niece, Prince George and Princess Charlotte

bouquet were forget-me-nots, a favourite of Harry's late mother Princess Diana, and a sprig of myrtle, a flower which symbolises love and marriage. The inclusion of myrtle in royal bouquets has been a tradition since the days of Queen Victoria, when it featured in the wedding bouquet of her daughter Princess Victoria in 1858. The plant which supplies the myrtle for the bouquets grows in the garden of Osborne House on the Isle of Wight, one of Queen Victoria's residences, and was originally brought from Germany, a gift from the grandmother of her husband Prince Albert.

In the absence of her father to give her away, Meghan took the brave decision to enter the chapel alone, save for her little bridesmaids and pageboys, including the twin sons of her close friend Jessica Mulroney who carried her train as she processed down the aisle to Handel's 'Eternal Source of Light Divine' sung by Welsh soprano Elin Manahan Thomas. Prince Charles was pleased to accept Meghan's request for him to stand in for her father – a sign of her full acceptance into the family – and it was Charles who took her arm halfway along the aisle. As Meghan took her place next to Prince Harry, he mouthed the words

'Thank you, Pa' to his father, followed by, to a beaming Meghan, 'You look amazing. I missed you.' He then lifted his bride's veil to reveal her face, lightly made up, with the delightful freckles she refuses to conceal clearly on view.

The Dean of Windsor David Connor conducted the greeting and gave a short and moving reminder on the meaning of marriage, leading into the first hymn 'Lord of All Hopefulness' and the declarations led by the Archbishop of Canterbury Justin Welby. These, as might be expected for a modern marriage, were unusual and touching with the addition of vows made by the congregation to support and uphold the couple, through the unanimous response: 'We will.'

With Meghan's train stretching spectacularly along the aisle, the bride and groom sat to listen to Harry's aunt – his mother Diana's sister Lady Jane Fellowes – give a reading, followed by a performance of the Thomas Tallis anthem 'If Ye Love Me' by the choir of St George's.

WEDDING GIFTS … AND TITLES

Rather than wedding gifts, Harry and Meghan requested their guests donate to charities. While they had no direct links to the charities selected, those charities did reflect their personal interests, including homelessness, HIV awareness and support, gender equality, conservation, the armed forces and sport.

From The Queen, the couple received a more intangible gift of not one but three titles. Following their wedding, Harry took the title of HRH the Duke of Sussex, Earl of Dumbarton and Baron Kilkeel, thereby making Meghan HRH the Duchess of Sussex, Countess of Dumbarton and Baroness Kilkeel respectively. These titles reflect the countries making up the United Kingdom of England, Scotland and Northern Ireland. Harry is only the second Duke of Sussex, the first being Prince Augustus Frederick, the sixth son of King George III, who held the title from 1801 until his death in 1843.

As anticipated, this was no conventional royal wedding. The Most Reverend Michael Curry gave an animated and powerful address on the subject of love. Reverend Curry, the first African American to be elected as presiding bishop and primate of the Episcopal Church in America, was invited by Meghan and Harry to participate in the ceremony. A charismatic figure, he is well-known for his strong views on discrimination and he opened his address with the words of race activist Martin Luther King.

A tender moment as Harry lifts Meghan's veil

Continuing the African-American theme, there followed a stirring performance of the Ben E. King song 'Stand by Me' by gospel singers the Kingdom Choir, before the exchange of the rings. Meghan's band, made of Welsh gold, as is traditional for royal wedding rings, and Harry's textured platinum ring were blessed by the Archbishop, before the couple made the traditional declarations of commitment. At precisely 12.40pm, to the cheers of the jubilant crowds outside, Meghan and Harry were declared husband and wife.

The register signed, Harry and Meghan left the chapel, pausing at the top of its dramatic steps for their equivalent of the traditional 'balcony kiss', while the State Trumpeters performed a celebratory fanfare. Next the newlyweds stepped into a horse-drawn Ascot Landau, built in 1883 for Queen Victoria; accompanied by two outriders and members of the Household Cavalry, the procession gave the public the opportunity to see the happy couple as they travelled through the streets of Windsor before returning to the castle through the picturesque Great Park.

The chapel bells continued to ring as a photo session took place in Windsor Castle's private garden, followed by the wedding breakfast, a luncheon hosted by The Queen in St George's Hall. In keeping with the non-traditional theme of the wedding, this was a buffet, served in bowls so guests could easily carry their food

The new Duke and Duchess of Sussex set off from St George's Chapel in the Ascot Landau carriage

and mingle. During the reception Harry asked Sir Elton John to perform four songs, pre-empted with the words, 'Can anyone play the piano?' Sir Elton was a friend of Princess Diana and his performance, which included 'Your Song' and 'I'm Still Standing', was a special, personal touch, another way of including Harry's late mother in the day's proceedings.

Celebrations continued with an evening reception for 200 guests at Frogmore House on the Windsor Estate, with an all-organic dinner, hosted by the Prince of Wales. Meghan, now dressed in an elegant Stella McCartney gown and wearing one of Princess Diana's favourite rings, smiled radiantly as she stepped into the open-top Jaguar E-Type Concept Zero – registration number E190518 to reflect the date – that Harry drove from the castle to Frogmore. The vehicle, originally manufactured in 1968, had been converted to run on electric power.

Speeches were given, including one, in a break with tradition, by Meghan who thanked her new father-in-law for welcoming her into the family. The night ended with dancing: Harry and Meghan took the lead, choosing Whitney Houston's

'I Wanna Dance with Somebody (Who Loves Me)' as their first dance. Finally, for any guests who were still hungry, gourmet burgers, pizza and candyfloss were served at midnight, while fireworks lit up the sky.

It was perhaps Harry who, in his speech, summed up what everyone had been thinking. Turning to his new wife, he praised her for navigating 'with such grace' what had been a stressful and pressured week. He then added quite simply, 'We make such a great team. I can't wait to spend the rest of my life with you.'

ABOVE: Claire Ptak from London-based bakery Violet Cakes and her team of six bakers spent five days making the lemon elderflower wedding cake

BELOW: Meghan and Harry leave Windsor Castle to head off to their evening reception at Frogmore House

A Royal Fashion Icon

In the weeks leading up to Meghan's marriage to Harry, fevered speculation grew as to the identity of the designer or fashion house tasked with creating that most important element of any woman's wedding day – the dress. What fuelled the intense discussion in Meghan's case was the fact that she is known to be a fan of high fashion and has a liking for female designers. Furthermore, her influence was already being felt by fashion labels and, therefore, to win the commission to design the wedding gown would be seen as something of a coup. That honour fell to Clare Waight Keller of Givenchy, who designed the wedding dress, and also to Stella McCartney for the evening reception gown, both being women designers at the top

OPPOSITE: On 22 May 2018, just days after her wedding, Meghan chose an elegant Philip Treacy hat when she attended Prince Charles's 70th birthday garden party at Buckingham Palace

of the tree in what used to be a mainly male-dominated industry. With Meghan's views on gender equality, it is perhaps unsurprising that she chose female talents, both of them British, to design two of the most important dresses that she will ever wear.

Meghan's interest in fashion started at an early age and, as she grew into adulthood, she developed her own sense of style. Upholding her principles, she dressed to please herself, rather than others, as a way of expressing her personality and herself as an individual.

While appreciating the craftsmanship and quality of designer items, Meghan has never been afraid to try high-street brands, in both cases creating an elegant mix of California laid-back cool and Hollywood glamour, more often than not accessorised by her trademark blow-dried hair and pointed stilettos. Even when wearing the simple outfit of white 'husband shirt' designed by her friend Misha Nonoo, torn skinny jeans, black pumps and sunglasses, as she did at the Invictus Games in 2017, Meghan can exude the same simple yet chic elegance that in the past has been associated with great style icons such as Audrey Hepburn and Jackie Kennedy Onassis albeit, thanks to the jeans, with a modern twist firmly rooted in the 21st century.

As a Hollywood actress, on the red carpet Meghan always kept her outfits tasteful and appropriate to the occasion, while capturing a very feminine look that was flattering to her petite frame. With her innate sense of style, she perfected the art of looking fabulous so

THE TIG

In The Tig, the popular lifestyle blog that Meghan wrote when she was a single woman, she made it clear that, in her view, dressing nicely and wearing make-up was in no way a contradiction in terms with being a feminist. Rather it was about making the most of yourself and feeling good, and if other people liked it too, then that was simply an added bonus.

Meghan looked cute and cool in a white 'husband shirt', designed by her friend Misha Nonoo, and torn skinny jeans at the Invictus Games 2017

that she attracted attention for the right reasons, resisting the temptation to wear the outrageous or overly revealing garments favoured by some female celebrities.

Like most women, over the years Meghan's personal style has evolved as she has herself matured from youthful ingénue to a sophisticated woman comfortable in her own skin. Since her marriage, her 'working wardrobe' has developed into elegant looks featuring plain tonal colours, chic in their simplicity and refinement. She fully understands the expectation, incumbent upon her as a senior royal, which is to appear professional at all times, while also following the style etiquette set out by her grandmother-in-law The Queen. These guidelines include knee-length hemlines, nude-coloured tights, small-brimmed hats that will not obscure the face or distract the eye of the onlooker, simple shoes (preferably in a neutral colour) and small bags or clutches. Trousers tend to be discouraged for formal engagements, unless appropriate to the occasion.

For a reception at Auckland War Memorial Museum in October 2018, Meghan chose this navy double-breasted dress with asymmetric hemline by Antonio Berardi, paired with nude heels by Aquazzura

CELEBRITY PRIVILEGE

As a well-known actress, Meghan would certainly have been either given or lent garments by leading designers, especially for red-carpet events which inevitably give valuable publicity for the designer in question. However, now that Meghan is a member of the Royal Family, the addition of these 'gifts' to her wardrobe will have come to an end as, in her position, she is prohibited from accepting them. If outfits are needed for public appearances, they are sent to her and laid out by her aides so that she can try on any that catch her eye prior to purchase.

Certainly, Meghan has changed her style to fit her new status since her marriage and is now more regularly seen with longer skirts, covered arms, sleek dresses that enhance her figure without being too revealing, and court shoes, as opposed to the high-heeled open sandals she previously favoured. Similarly, the large tote bags she used to carry are more often replaced by small handbags, while one or two exquisite pieces now take the place of numerous items of costume jewellery.

To help her find her way through the minefield of royal fashion diktats, Meghan has a small team of stylists and advisers. Whilst Meghan selects the clothes that she likes, they advise on their suitability for the occasion in question, an important

consideration when all eyes are fixed upon her as a high-profile member of the Royal Family and opinions as to her choice, both in favour and against, are freely given in the media. However, more than once Meghan has managed to push the boundaries of tradition while remaining within royal protocol, such as her selection of an off-the-shoulder pink two-piece by Carolina Herrera for the Trooping the Colour ceremony in 2018. While her daring neckline caused some eyebrows to be raised, the reliable advice of her aides would have ensured that no disrespect was shown either to The Queen or to the event itself.

As Meghan continues to adjust to her life as Duchess of Sussex, she will, no doubt, develop and refine her personal style over time. In keeping with her current ethos, she is likely to continue to favour designers from Britain, the USA and Canada, particularly if they are female; and as designers in Commonwealth countries come to the fore in greater numbers over the coming decades, she may choose to wear more of their work also.

The power of the 'Meghan effect' should not be underestimated. It has added millions of pounds to the fashion economy, not only in the UK but also in North America where she has many followers. So powerful is Meghan's influence that any garment she is seen wearing can sell out within hours of her appearance, while other labels – often high-street brands – offering similar styles also benefit as women seek the 'Meghan look' on a budget. Even Marks & Spencer's simple bell-sleeved black jumper, priced at £45, which Meghan wore on her

> The power of the 'Meghan effect' should not be underestimated

visit to Brixton prior to her marriage, sold out twice, requiring the company to go into overdrive in an effort to restock as quickly as possible to meet demand. Equally, the striking Ralph Lauren blue-and-white striped shirt, teamed with white trousers, that the recently married Meghan wore at Wimbledon in 2018 led to fans scouring shops and the internet for similar items to create their own version of this elegantly classic look.

OPPOSITE: Newly-wed Meghan matched her pink dress by Carolina Herrera with a Philip Treacy hat at Trooping the Colour 2018

CLOCKWISE FROM TOP LEFT: In a cool 1950s-style Carolina Herrera dress, Meghan arrives to watch Harry play in a charity polo match

In Tonga, and elegant in a Veronica Beard blue shirt-dress

Meghan's statement gold earrings were the perfect accessory for her plain green shift dress in Fiji

This blush-pink sleeveless trench dress was by Canadian label House of Nonie

OPPOSITE (CLOCKWISE FROM TOP LEFT): In Australia, Meghan wore a sundress by American eco-friendly brand Reformation

Meghan in a Dior dress with bateau neckline – similar to that of her wedding dress – at Westminster Abbey, July 2018

Meghan in a stunning Club Monaco dress at the wedding of friends Charlie van Straubenzee and Daisy Jenks

A glowing Meghan, in a peplum top, at a service marking the centenary of the Armistice, November 2018

Meghan and her sister-in-law Catherine at Wimbledon 2018 with Gill Brook, wife of the Wimbledon chairman. Meghan chose an oversized blue-and-white striped shirt, high-waisted wide-leg white trousers, both by Ralph Lauren, and Maison Michel straw hat, while Catherine's patterned dress was by Jenny Packham.

Prince Harry's mother Diana was known for her beauty and love of fashion. In Meghan, Harry now has another beautiful and stylish woman in his life who, like Diana, is constantly photographed and discussed by the media. As the public's fascination and enthusiasm for Meghan continues, the clothes she chooses remain under close scrutiny by conventional media and bloggers alike – as was evident during her pregnancy.

In the relatively recent past, royal women – and, indeed, women generally – sought to disguise their pregnancy with smock-style dresses, but Meghan displayed her modern outlook by celebrating her condition, rather than attempting to hide it, and she was often seen cradling her bump affectionately.

In the second trimester of her pregnancy, Meghan selected clothes that were flattering to a smaller bump, such as the black, bow-belted Stella McCartney coat she wore to the Festival of Remembrance on 10 November 2018. The next day, for the Service of Remembrance at Westminster Abbey, it was a navy Prada outfit: the peplum top covered her tummy, while the sleek bodice and skirt accentuated her slim figure, and the bateau neckline drew the eye to her face.

On other occasions, as her pregnancy progressed, her bump was clearly visible. Stretchy fabrics offered both support and comfort, and outfits on or below the knee provided balance and elegance. When coupled with a smart, loose fitting coat, such as the Brock Collection floral dress and Soia

A week before Christmas 2018, Meghan visited Brinsworth House in Twickenham, a retirement home for those who have worked in the entertainment industry

and Kyo grey coat she wore in December 2018 to the Royal Variety Charity's Twickenham nursing home and the black Hatch dress and camel Oscar de la Renta coat pairing she chose for a visit to Smart Works in the following January, these figure-hugging dresses made a beautifully modern maternity-wear fashion statement, approved of and followed by other mothers-to-be. This winning style combination continued when Meghan, at the premiere of the film *The Wider Earth*, looked stunning in a slim-fitting white Calvin Klein turtleneck dress worn with a loose white Amanda Wakeley coat, perfectly offset by a beehive bun hairstyle.

Meghan displayed her modern outlook by celebrating her condition

The Duchess of Sussex, wearing a flowing blue kaftan, with the King of Morocco at his residence in Rabat

Meghan chose a vibrant colour combination, with matching high heels, when she visited Birkenhead on the Wirral in January 2019

Meghan has always ensured that her clothing is appropriate for the occasion, her stylish dressing undiminished by her pregnancy. In February 2019, on her official trip to Morocco, a Muslim country, loose styles were perfect, including the stunning red caped dress by Valentino that ensured the right first impression for her arrival in Casablanca, and the long Carolina Herrera kaftan she wore when meeting King Mohammed VI in Rabat.

While Meghan has tended to be drawn towards neutral colours, she has, on occasion, selected statement outfits in vibrant hues, as well as designs a little different from her usual look. In a colour clash favoured by Princess Diana, the purple dress combined with a scarlet coat on a visit to Birkenhead in January made for a spectacular winter outfit, while her floaty dress for a visit to Bristol was almost bohemian in appearance – a style unusual for Meghan but it worked perfectly.

For off-duty maternity wear, Meghan remained true to her tried-and-tested skinny jeans and T-shirts, accompanied by season-appropriate jackets and coats, with occasional forays into sportswear tops and leggings. Occasionally, she swapped her beloved high heels for flat loafers, pumps and even trainers.

Despite being pregnant, Meghan attended numerous evening functions and at these she excelled when it came to putting together a maternity outfit. In February 2019, at the Endeavour Fund Awards, Meghan demonstrated that a simple white shirt worn with a long black skirt can be the ultimate in classic chic, even when seven months pregnant. At other evening events, both the Givenchy one-shoulder gown she wore for the Fashion Awards 2018 and the blue sequinned Roland Mouret dress she chose for a charity performance of Cirque du Soleil oozed pure glamour.

Following the birth of her child, Meghan's fashion fans eagerly await her take on style as a new mother with a baby to attend to. One thing is certain – it will be a look that combines practicality as a mother with Meghan's inimitable sense of style.

Her baby's arrival just a few weeks away, Meghan, dressed in Givenchy, chats to guests at the Endeavour Fund Awards in London, February 2019

A Year as Duchess

Meghan's first year as Duchess of Sussex was not only extremely busy, it was also marked by a change in status when, following the birth of her first baby, she became a mother.

Her busy year began immediately after her marriage, with her first public appearance as a royal wife being made just three days following her wedding when she attended a Buckingham Palace garden party held in honour of her new father-in-law Prince Charles to celebrate his patronages, charitable interests and military affiliations ahead of his 70th birthday in November 2018. Other appearances included Royal Ascot in June and, in the same month, Trooping the Colour, a parade of the regiments of the British and Commonwealth armies that has annually marked the reigning sovereign's official birthday since 1748. It was at the latter event that Meghan had her first experience of riding in a horse-drawn carriage along The Mall to Horse Guards Parade to watch the formal ceremony and afterwards standing on the famous Buckingham Palace balcony with other members of the Royal Family to wave to the cheering crowds below.

Not all public appearances have been so high-profile, as Meghan accompanied her husband on several visits to smaller events. One of these was attending a performance of the musical *Hamilton* at the Victoria Palace Theatre in London's West End, in aid of Harry's Lesotho charity Sentebale and Coach Core, a charitable sport coaching apprenticeship scheme supported by the Royal Foundation.

ABOVE: The Duchess of Sussex stands alongside her in-laws, the Duke and Duchess of Cornwall, while her husband makes a speech at Prince Charles's 70th birthday garden party at Buckingham Palace

OPPOSITE: The Duchess of Sussex on 14 June 2018, the day she visited Chester Town Hall with Her Majesty The Queen

The Duke and Duchess of Sussex at Trooping the Colour, June 2018

According to Harry, the gala performance raised 'a huge amount of money' for the causes, while, on meeting the cast, Meghan, in relaxed mood, teased her husband by revealing to the actors that her husband 'couldn't stop singing the songs'.

One visit that did attract public attention was Meghan's first official engagement with Harry's grandmother. Meghan has proved a great success with her new family and The Queen has quickly become very fond of her, not least through their shared love of animals, and dogs in particular. The first sign of Meghan's growing bond with Her Majesty came at Christmas 2017, prior to Meghan's marriage, when she was invited to join the celebrations at Sandringham in Norfolk, something previously unheard of for a non-royal, as Meghan was at the time, albeit that she and Harry were engaged. While The Queen may have been acknowledging that Meghan would have otherwise been alone during the festive season, with no family nearby, it was nevertheless a significant deviation from the norm. In return, Meghan seems to have developed a great admiration and respect for The Queen, speaking of her in glowing terms as 'an incredible woman', not only

The Duke and Duchess of Sussex meet the cast following a charity gala performance of the musical *Hamilton* in London

when it comes to her relationship with Harry but also in recognition of her achievements as monarch throughout the many decades.

This first official engagement with The Queen came relatively early on in Meghan's marriage, another sign of how comfortable Her Majesty feels in Meghan's company. The two women travelled together to north-west England on the royal locomotive – a special honour as it is believed that neither the Duke and Duchess of Cambridge nor Prince Harry have ever been on board the by-invitation-only

A month to the day after her wedding, Meghan was at Royal Ascot wearing a stylish hat by Philip Treacy

train – which, within its nine carriages, contains a 12-seater dining room, en suite bedrooms and a luxuriously decorated saloon. On their arrival in Runcorn, Cheshire, The Queen, with Meghan at her side, opened the Mersey Gateway Bridge and Chester's Storyhouse Theatre. While our sovereign expects to see enthusiastic crowds wherever she goes, it is an experience to which Meghan has had to rapidly become accustomed.

Less than a month after her wedding, Meghan joined The Queen on a royal visit to Cheshire

A panoramic view of Great Tew in the Cotswolds

Royal Homes

Having become a family of three, Meghan and Harry moved from the quaint two-bedroom Nottingham Cottage in the grounds of Kensington Palace to their very own marital home, a gift to them from The Queen: Frogmore Cottage in the Home Park on the Windsor Estate. It had been thought that the pair would move into Apartment 1 of Kensington Palace, next door to William and his wife Catherine, but following a decision for the brothers to separate their royal courts and households, a move further out from the capital away from the public eye was the favoured option for Meghan, Harry and their new baby.

Windsor has a special place in their hearts, not least because their wedding took place within the castle walls, with the reception held at nearby Frogmore House. Being just 20 miles from London, the ten-bedroom house combines ease of accessibility to the city, where their office remains at Kensington Palace, with private and tranquil surroundings, making it an ideal location for the couple who have vowed to give their child – or children – as normal a way of life as possible.

Having been previously used for staff accommodation, their Berkshire residence underwent extensive renovation, to include a yoga studio and nursery, turning it into a modern family home.

In 2018, the couple leased a converted barn in the picturesque village of Great Tew in Oxfordshire as a country retreat for relaxed weekends away. The village sits in a 4,000-acre estate, owned by the Johnston family who are keen conservationists, both in terms of the estate's natural environment and the traditional properties to

FROGMORE

Meghan and Harry's new ten-bedroom home of Frogmore Cottage is set in the grounds of the grand and lavish Frogmore House on the Windsor Estate. The original Great and Little Frogmore Estates were bought by Henry VIII in the 16th century, with the name of Frogmore being derived from the large numbers of frogs that inhabit the marshy land surrounding the house. The original house was built by Charles II in 1680–84 but it was Queen Charlotte, wife of George III, having purchased the lease in 1792, who carried out extensive work to turn it into a real royal home, a place where she and her unmarried daughters could relax and enjoy the beauty of the house and its surroundings. Charlotte's love of botany and flowers is reflected not only in the design of the gardens but also in the interior decoration, in particular the Mary Moser Room which contains beautiful wall and ceiling artwork created for Queen Charlotte by the famous floral artist of that name.

Following Charlotte's death, the house remained popular with members of the Royal Family over the generations and it was the home of the Duchess of Kent, mother of Queen Victoria, for nearly 20 years. Queen Victoria herself visited the house frequently and on her death in 1901 she was interred next to her beloved husband Prince Albert in the mausoleum she had had built for them on the west side of the gardens. In 1928, grounds south of the mausoleum were consecrated and since then other members of the Royal Family have been buried in what became the Frogmore Royal Burial Ground, including Edward VIII, the Queen's uncle, who famously abdicated the throne to marry Wallis Simpson.

Currently, no member of the Royal Family lives in the house, but it continues to be used for entertaining and special occasions, such as wedding receptions, as indeed it was for Meghan and Harry's evening wedding reception.

Meghan and Harry's first home together was Nottingham Cottage in the grounds of Kensington Palace

Frogmore House and its grounds, where Meghan and Harry's new family home, Frogmore Cottage, is situated

be found upon it. Among Meghan and Harry's neighbours are Victoria and David Beckham, journalist and television presenter Jeremy Clarkson, and former UK Prime Minister David Cameron and his wife Samantha.

First Official Tour

Following Harry's appointment as Youth Ambassador to the Commonwealth in April 2018, it perhaps was not surprising that the newlyweds' first official tour was to a part of the world where The Queen remains Head of State and is highly regarded. In mid October, the young couple arrived in Sydney, Australia, for the start of a 16-day visit to Australasia that included stops in four countries and involved 76 engagements.

Meghan in the grounds of Admiralty House in Sydney on the day the news that she was expecting her first child was made public

While Meghan had already experienced a taste of public appearances within the UK, this visit was to provide an introduction to the hectic timetabling and the special cultural displays and performances associated with these types of tours for members of the Royal Family.

First, however, at the very start of this trip, came a very important announcement. On 15 October, shortly after the couple had landed in Sydney, Kensington Palace let it be known through its official Twitter page that Meghan was expecting her first child, a modern mode of communication for this thoroughly modern pair.

With this exciting news made public, the crowds who turned out to see Meghan and Harry at every stage of their trip passed on their congratulations, with their first baby gifts being presented on their arrival at Admiralty House in Sydney. A cuddly kangaroo toy and a tiny pair of Ugg boots, both quintessentially Australian, were presents from the Governor-General Sir Peter Cosgrove who acts as The Queen's representative in Australia.

The focus of the tour was youth leadership, as well as environmental and conservation efforts, but Harry's work with injured servicemen through the Invictus Games was also an important part of it. With this in mind, the main business on the first day was to meet representatives from the 18 countries taking part in the Sydney Invictus Games, which Harry was due to open and close during the tour.

Following the announcement that Meghan and Harry are to become parents, they were delighted with gifts of baby Ugg boots and a toy kangaroo

ABOVE: Harry and Meghan engage with children at Albert Park Primary School in Melbourne

RIGHT: At Taronga Zoo in Sydney, the Duke and Duchess of Sussex met koalas, two of whom were named Meghan and Harry in celebration of the royal couple's wedding

OPPOSITE (CLOCKWISE FROM TOP LEFT): Meghan and Harry lay a wreath at the official opening of an extension to the Anzac Memorial at Hyde Park, Sydney, where a plaque reads: 'This memorial extension was opened by a grandson of the Queen on the 25th October 2018'

Meghan wore an Emilia Wickstead dress and Philip Treacy hat for the Anzac Memorial ceremony

The Duke and Duchess of Sussex cheer on competitors in a sailing event at the 2018 Invictus Games in Sydney harbour

The Duke and Duchess of Sussex help prepare food for the animals during a visit to a farm in Dubbo

The rain did not deter the Duke and Duchess of Sussex when they visited Victoria Park in Dubbo

This initial stay in Sydney was short as the next day saw Meghan and Harry travelling some 185 miles to the small town of Dubbo, where they were to see for themselves the effects of long-lasting drought on the farming community there. Ironically, no sooner had they arrived than the heavens opened forcing Harry to address his audience of locals from the shelter of a large umbrella, much to everyone's amusement.

On arrival at Dubbo airport, the Duchess received a welcoming hug from this small boy

The famous Australian sun was also in hiding the following day when the couple arrived in a cloudy Melbourne. At the beach they talked to members of an initiative called Beach Patrol, which helps keep the area clean, before later visiting a primary school where the children take lunch boxes containing foods free of packaging. In recognition of these conservation efforts and to demonstrate her awareness of sustainability issues, during her visit Meghan chose to wear a stylish pair of flat shoes, albeit with an important difference. Made by Rothy's, the shoes were unusual in that the knitted uppers were made completely from sterilised plastic water bottles that had been repurposed into a yarn.

From Melbourne, it was back to Sydney, where Harry climbed the famous harbour bridge – alongside a number of Invictus athletes and Australian Prime Minister Scott Morrison – to raise the Invictus flag prior to the launch of the Games. The couple also visited the famous Bondi Beach, where barefoot and decked in a floral lei garland, Meghan was delighted to meet fellow yoga practitioners. Harry has spoken at length about his interest in helping people with mental health

ABOVE: It was a windy day when Meghan and Harry met life-savers on South Melbourne Beach

RIGHT: A garlanded Meghan on Bondi Beach

Meghan and Harry at an official welcome ceremony in Fiji, where they unveiled a statue of British-Fijian war hero Sergeant Talaiasi Labalaba

issues and it was here that the pair met One Wave, a surfing community group that raises awareness of mental health and wellbeing in innovative ways, and joined in an 'anti bad vibes' circle during the group's 'Fluro Friday' session for which members wear fluorescent and brightly coloured garments.

With visits to schools, attendance at the opening of the Anzac Memorial Centenary Extension and visits to the Invictus Games events, Meghan and Harry's few days in Sydney were hectic before they headed off on day seven to Fraser Island in Queensland for the dedication of a Queen's Commonwealth Canopy forestry project. The next day was spent in Suva in Fiji, where they attended a traditional welcome ceremony. Here, again, climate change and sustainability were very much to the fore, with a second Queen's Commonwealth Canopy dedication and a performance by students on the effects of global warming.

Meghan has always been interested in women's issues and while in Fiji she learnt about a number of women's organisations in the country, in particular the

Meghan was presented with a colourful garland to go over her pretty pink print dress, by artisan fashion label Figue, when she attended a morning reception at the British High Commissioner's residence in Suva, Fiji

UN Women project Markets for Change, which promotes female empowerment across the Pacific islands. It was in relation to this that Meghan undertook her only solo visit during the tour when she visited Suva market to meet female vendors working within the project, before going on to give an inspirational speech at the University of the South Pacific on the empowerment of women and female education in developing countries.

From Fiji, the next stop was Tonga, where, again, the couple received a traditional welcome Tongan style, as well as being entertained by children at Tupou College, where the boys' choir reduced Meghan to tears of laughter with their song about mosquitoes, aimed at keeping the zika virus, which has affected this part of the world, at bay. Zika, if caught by a pregnant woman, can cause a baby to be born with the condition microcephalus; however, despite her being pregnant, following a full risk assessment, it was considered safe for the Duchess to travel to the region as the visit was to last less than 24 hours.

LEFT: Meghan and Harry wear ta'ovala, traditional Tongan dress, on their visit to Fa'onelua Convention Centre to see an exhibition of Tongan handicrafts

BELOW: Local people bid a fond farewell to the Duke and Duchess of Sussex at Fua'amotu International Airport as the royal couple leave Tonga

Like Fiji, Tonga has been badly affected by deforestation and so Harry and Meghan were delighted to be able to dedicate yet another forest to the Queen's Commonwealth Canopy in a project that aims to encourage indigenous species and discourage invasive ones.

The visit to Tonga was short as the couple had to return to Sydney for the

closing ceremony of the Invictus Games. Of course, the previous year's Games in Toronto had been important to the couple as it had been their first real public appearance together. The 2018 Games were significant in another way: Meghan, now as Harry's wife, was able to give her own speech, acknowledging the importance of the Games for injured service personnel and the bonds that form not only between competitors but between their families also, to create 'a camaraderie and close-knit sense of community which can only be defined as the Invictus Spirit', adding, 'I want to thank you all for welcoming me into the Invictus family.'

BELOW: The Duchess of Sussex congratulates the United States wheelchair basketball team who won gold at the Sydney Invictus Games

BOTTOM: The Duchess of Sussex gives an address during the closing ceremony of the Invictus Games in Sydney

OPPOSITE (CLOCKWISE FROM TOP LEFT):
The Duke and Duchess of Sussex arrive for the Your Commonwealth Youth Challenge reception at Marlborough House, London, July 2018

Meghan and Harry share a kiss at the Royal County of Berkshire Polo Club in Windsor, following a charity polo match in July 2018

The Duchess of Sussex signs the visitors' book at Edes House in Chichester, when she and Harry made their first joint official visit to Sussex in October 2018

The Duchess of Sussex shows her sporting prowess at the Coach Core Awards at Loughborough University, September 2018

THIS PAGE, TOP: A warm welcome from the crowds awaited Meghan on her visit to Sussex, October 2018

MIDDLE: The Duke and Duchess of Cambridge and the Duke and Duchess of Sussex arrive for the RAF Centenary service at Westminster Abbey, July 2018

BELOW LEFT: The Duchess of Sussex is greeted by President of Ireland Michael D. Higgins and his wife on the royal visit to Dublin, July 2018

BELOW: Meghan and Harry mingle with guests at a reception at Buckingham Palace to mark the centenary of the RAF

QUEEN'S COMMONWEALTH CANOPY

The Queen's Commonwealth Canopy (QCC) was launched in 2015 at the Commonwealth Heads of Government Meeting held in Malta. The idea behind it was to create a global network of forest conservation initiatives across the 53 Commonwealth countries that would not only create a lasting legacy to mark The Queen's position as head of the Commonwealth but would also save the precious indigenous forests of those countries for future generations.

The QCC brings together the 53 countries in a common cause, as they work to share knowledge and best practice. The initiative is led by the Royal Commonwealth Society in partnership with Cool Earth, a charity committed to stopping deforestation and climate change, and the Commonwealth Forestry Association that provides a science-based link between forestry experts and government policy makers.

At the end of 2018, 35 countries had either dedicated existing forests to the QCC or were planting new ones, with others expected to join. Each QCC forest is identified by a special dedication service; the first was held in Singapore and since then dedications have been held in countries as diverse as Belize, Australia, Brunei Darussalam, Canada, Fiji, Cyprus, Barbados and Malawi. Countries are not required to make a financial outlay to ensure the less affluent nations are not excluded.

The Queen has always had a keen interest in the conservation of woodlands and this was reflected in her Diamond Jubilee year of 2012 by the creation of the 460-acre National Forest in Leicestershire, in tandem with the planting of six million trees across the UK by the Woodland Trust. The Queen's Commonwealth Canopy can be seen as an extension of that passion and commitment.

Meghan receives a Maori greeting at the opening of Oceania at the Royal Academy of Arts in London in September 2018, prior to her visit to New Zealand

Another traditional Maori greeting for Meghan, this time during her visit to Te Papaiouru Marae, Ohinemutu, New Zealand on 31 October 2018

Leaving Sydney the day after the closure of the Invictus Games, another traditional welcome awaited Meghan and Harry as they arrived at their next destination – New Zealand; here they experienced the Maori haka. Meghan was also able to put into practice the hongi, the Maori greeting of pressing noses and foreheads together, something she had learnt to do in London a month before her visit when she opened the Oceania exhibition at the Royal Academy of Arts, celebrating art from Australia, New Zealand, Tonga and Fiji.

As they had done earlier in the tour, in New Zealand the couple focused on conservation, women's issues and mental health, with Meghan giving a heartfelt speech at Government House in Wellington, the country's capital situated on North Island, as part of the 125th anniversary of women's suffrage in the country. Other visits in the city included tea at the Maranui Café to meet representatives of mental health projects, in particular those supporting the Maori population and others working to tackle the high suicide rate in New Zealand among young people.

The Duchess of Sussex is a good sport and took part in a welly-wanging contest while in New Zealand

Auckland was the next stop, where a further Queen's Commonwealth Canopy forest area was dedicated and it was there that Meghan was introduced, by youngsters from the group Trees in Survival, to welly wanging, a rural traditional 'sport' that travelled to the southern hemisphere with English immigrants. With the couple on opposing teams, it was Meghan's who emerged victorious.

The following day, trees also featured on the couple's trip to Rotorua, where they visited Redwoods Treewalk, learnt about the park's trees and met members of the local cycling community. They were also informed about the kiwi breeding programme being conducted in the area; they talked with conservationists working to preserve this endangered species which has iconic status in the country and is its much-loved national symbol.

Meghan and Harry travelled home from Auckland, having completed a packed itinerary on what was deemed an extremely successful trip. During the tour, they had made a point of carrying out 'walkabouts', meeting the local people, chatting to them and sometimes even hugging them in the informal manner that has become the couple's trademark. Despite this being her first high-profile visit abroad, and with all eyes upon her, Meghan chatted with an easy charm to well-wishers of all ages and demonstrated the natural rapport she has with children. The success of the visit and the enthusiasm encountered by the couple did much to bolster the image of the Royal Family in this distant part of the world where The Queen is still regarded with great affection and loyalty.

LEFT: Meghan and Harry navigate a suspension bridge during a visit to Redwoods Treewalk in Rotorua, New Zealand

BELOW: The Duke and Duchess of Sussex are introduced to kiwi chicks at the Kiwi Breeding Programme at Rainbow Springs in Rotorua

ABOVE: The Duke and Duchess of Sussex wear traditional Maori cloaks (korowai) during a visit to Te Papaiouru, Ohinemutu, Rotorua, where they attended a lunch in their honour

RIGHT: With a painting of Queen Elizabeth II behind her, Meghan spoke at a reception in Wellington that marked the 125th anniversary of women's suffrage in New Zealand

OPPOSITE (CLOCKWISE FROM TOP LEFT): Meghan plants a tree at the dedication of an area of bush to the Queen's Commonwealth Canopy project in Redvale, New Zealand

During a walkabout in Rotorua, the Duchess of Sussex and a little girl share a hug

Meghan meets actors during a visit to Courtenay Creative in Wellington, which celebrates the city's arts scene

Hubb Community Kitchen

Although Meghan works alongside Harry on many projects and official visits, she is also undertaking her own and these will, no doubt, develop as she grows ever more familiar with her new country of domicile. One such project has been the Hubb Community Kitchen. The kitchen was set up by local women in the wake of London's Grenfell Tower disaster that, in June 2017, left 72 people dead, more than 70 injured and nearly 250 homeless. It aims to provide food and comfort to those affected by the fire, the name Hubb being a play on the English word for a centre and the Arabic word for love.

Initially, Meghan became involved by paying low-profile visits to the kitchen, helping with cooking, getting to know the women and chatting to local people at the Al Manaar Community Centre where the Hubb is based, in what was then the Duchess's home district of Kensington and Chelsea.

As the Duchess's interest in the project grew, the kitchen became very much her personal project and in September 2018 she attended a very special event in the gardens of Kensington Palace. Accompanied by her mother and husband, Meghan launched the kitchen's *Together: Our Community Cookbook*, a collection of favourite recipes enjoyed by the families of the women cooks at the Hubb, for which Meghan wrote a touching foreword. The Hubb was Meghan's first solo charitable project as Duchess, and at the launch she gave her first public speech as a member of the Royal Family. She acknowledged the power of food in overcoming problems, saying, 'When you get to know the story of the recipe, you get to know the person behind it … to celebrate what connects us rather than what divides us.'

Meghan was delighted to return to the centre in November 2018 to discover that through UK sales alone the book had already raised £210,000 and was a bestseller. Now supported by the Royal Foundation, the proceeds from the book have allowed the Hubb to refurbish its kitchen so that it can open seven days a week instead of two as it did formerly. It has also expanded its remit, to include the provision of a safe space for women suffering domestic abuse and the promotion of healthy eating for children.

It is intended that, through the Royal Foundation, the Hubb's work will be extended to allow similar projects be launched elsewhere.

On 20 September 2018, Meghan's mother, Doria Ragland, was at Kensington Palace to lend her support at the launch of the cookbook in aid of the Grenfell Tower disaster

The Duchess of Sussex wrote a foreword for the *Together* cookbook, held here by Zahira Ghaswala, one of the project's coordinators

Meghan helps pack food during a return visit to the Hubb Community Kitchen in November 2018

Christmas 2018

Christmas is always an important time for The Queen's family, and that of 2018 was Meghan's first as a married woman and as a full member of the Royal Family. For most spouses, their first royal Christmas comes after their marriage, but for Meghan, who had already attended as Harry's fiancée in 2017, the format and protocol came as no surprise.

Christmas started early with the traditional Queen's Christmas luncheon held at Buckingham Palace on 19 December 2018. As many members of the family as possible attend the lunch, which allows The Queen to see both those who will spend the festive season with her at Sandringham and those who will be absent, so it has become a major event in the royal calendar, particularly as the family has expanded over the years.

A few days later, it was time to set off for Sandringham House for the Christmas celebrations proper. Tradition plays a major role in the royal festivities and these start on Christmas Eve with the final touches being made to the grand Christmas tree, followed by a formal meal with black tie dress code and, in the German tradition, the exchanging of gifts, which, as Royal Family custom dictates, must be inexpensive and preferably amusing.

Christmas Day rituals start at 8.30am when the men have a cooked breakfast together, while their wives enjoy a light breakfast in their rooms. The Queen likes to give as many staff as possible the day off, so in contrast to the rest of the country, meals throughout the rest of Christmas Day are relatively light and include a cold buffet, with watching The Queen's Speech at 3pm on television a must for all.

One of the most important traditions is attending St Mary Magdalene Church on the Sandringham Estate, where the Royal Family, with the exception of The Queen and Prince Philip who come by car (although he did not attend in 2018), arrive on foot at 11am for the service. Hundreds of well-wishers gather in the grounds of the church to wave and perhaps catch a word or two with the royals both before and after the service.

LEFT: Christmas 2018: The Duchess of Sussex greets the crowds as she arrive for the Christmas Day service at St Mary Magdalene Church at Sandringham

OPPOSITE: The Prince of Wales, the Duke and Duchess of Cambridge and the Duke and Duchess of Sussex arrive for the Christmas Day church service

Boxing Day for the Royal Family traditionally features a hearty breakfast followed by game shooting on the estate, but Meghan, as a passionate animal lover, did not partake in this event. Once the shooting party had returned from their day's sport, the 'Boxing Day feast' of cold cuts was enjoyed before everyone departed for their respective homes.

That Meghan has been fully accepted into the Royal Family was left in no doubt by the fact that she and Harry had the honour of being invited by The Queen to stay in Sandringham House itself for their first Christmas as a married couple. In 2017, when they were engaged, they had stayed at Anmer Hall, the Norfolk home of Harry's brother William and his wife Catherine, but now, with an increase in status as a full member of the Royal Family, Meghan was able to experience a true Sandringham Christmas as an 'insider', the first of many to come.

Royal support

As soon as her pregnancy was announced, Meghan made it clear that she intended to continue working for as long as possible and, indeed, in 2019, she had a busy few months prior to the birth of her baby. During this time Meghan began to further consolidate her interests, as evidenced by the type of organisations that she and Harry chose to visit.

Meghan's first official outing in 2019 was to Birkenhead and Wirral, on Merseyside, where, with Harry, she visited several local projects, including Tomorrow's Women Wirral that works with disadvantaged and vulnerable women. While in Birkenhead, the couple admired a poignant bronze statue depicting an

exhausted First World War soldier, unveiled in November 2018 to mark the centenary of war poet Wilfred Owen, who lived there as a child.

Other visits early in 2019 included a special performance at the Royal Albert

LEFT: This handwritten message of support from Meghan made its way into a food parcel prepared by her for the One25 charity in Bristol

ABOVE: The Duke and Duchess of Sussex in Birkenhead, alongside the commemorative statue entitled *Futility* after one of Wilfred Owen's poems

Hall in London of *Totem* by the Cirque du Soleil in aid of Harry's Sentebale charity and a day in Bristol. During this latter visit, as well as braving snow showers to meet local people on a walkabout, Meghan and Harry visited a young people's boxing charity gym and the Bristol Old Vic theatre. The same day, on an unannounced visit to One25, a charity that helps females escape life on the streets, Meghan – inspired by a method employed by a school lunch programme in the US – wrote messages of empowerment on the bananas contained in the food parcels supplied to the women using the charity's services.

In late February, the royal couple travelled to Morocco for a short official visit aimed at consolidating the relationship between the UK and the North African country. The highlight of the three-day tour was a visit to a girls' school in the town of Asni in the Atlas Mountains, where Meghan talked to the girls about their aspirations, sometimes speaking to them in French, a gesture greatly appreciated by all those present.

Soon after her return from Morocco, on 8 March Meghan joined an impressive line-up of prominent women activists and leaders at a panel discussion to mark International Women's Day. The event, hosted by The Queen's Commonwealth Trust of which Her Majesty has made Meghan vice-president, gave the Duchess the chance to speak out on gender equality issues, her passion for the topic summed up in her quote '… it would be impossible for me to sit back and not do anything about it.'

> … it would be impossible for me to sit back and not do anything about it.

With her heartfelt commitment to her causes, in her first year as the Duchess of Sussex, Meghan showed that she is a royal who is truly making a difference.

ABOVE: The Duchess of Sussex admires the gift of a henna tattoo – a token of luck for her and her new baby – at the 'Education For All' boarding house in Asni during the royal tour of Morocco

RIGHT: On 5 March 2019, Meghan and Harry chat to his aunt, the Princess Royal, at a reception to mark the 50th anniversary year of the investiture of the Prince of Wales

PATRONAGES

During her first year as the Duchess of Sussex, Meghan took her first steps to becoming a royal patron of charities and organisations in areas specific to her interests. It is usual for members of the Royal Family to offer patronage in this way and, for any organisation, it is a tremendous privilege that gives a positive boost to its image, raising its public profile and providing value-added confidence and credibility.

Meghan is patron of the Royal National Theatre, a patronage she took over from The Queen; animal welfare charity Mayhew that also supports impoverished and homeless pet owners; Smart Works, which helps disadvantaged women enter or return to the workplace; and the Association of Commonwealth Universities that aims to provide higher education to all citizens across the Commonwealth. As with the National Theatre, this latter patronage, by way of an affirmation of Meghan's work, was passed on to her by The Queen.

LEFT: Meghan with other panellists at the International Women's Day discussion held at King's College, London, where she vowed her baby will be a feminist 'whether it be a boy or a girl'

Awaiting baby

In the weeks leading up to the birth of her baby, there was much press speculation about which would be Meghan's last public appearance before the happy event.

A busy 24 hours for Meghan was Commonwealth Day 2019 which fell on 11 March, and marked the 70th anniversary of the modern Commonwealth. She and Harry started the day at Canada House in London where they attended an event that celebrated the diverse community of young Canadians living and working in the UK and recognised their positive contributions to British society. Later the couple were at Westminster Abbey with other members of the Royal Family – including The Queen, the Duke and Duchess of Cornwall, the Duke and Duchess of Cambridge, and the Duke of York – for the Commonwealth Day service, the largest annual inter-faith gathering in the UK.

A Palace spokesperson said that this concluded Meghan's public engagements prior to the baby's arrival 'but she is not on maternity leave yet', confirming that the Duchess would 'continue working privately behind the scenes, taking meetings' and 'using this period to catch up with those involved in her patronage-related endeavours'.

However, following the attacks on worshippers at mosques in Christchurch, New Zealand on 15 March, the Duke and Duchess of Sussex represented the Royal Family when they visited New Zealand House in London to lay flowers and sign a book of condolence. Meghan wrote, 'Our deepest condolences ... We are with you'; and under their names, Harry added 'Arohanui', which is Maori for 'With deep affection'.

It was a sombre moment of reflection as they reached out to the nation that had taken them to their hearts during their royal visit in October 2018.

The Duke and Duchess of Sussex and the Duke and Duchess of Cambridge at Westminster Abbey for the Commonwealth Day 2019 service

Before attending the Commonwealth Day service at Westminster Abbey on 11 March 2019, the Duke and Duchess of Sussex delighted youngsters they met at a youth event at Canada House in London. For the occasion, Meghan wore a coat with matching dress by Canadian-born designer Erdem Moralioglu

A Royal Baby Boy

Meghan had a healthy pregnancy as evidenced by her overseas trips to Morocco and New York in the last few weeks before her baby was born, the latter for a baby shower hosted by her American friends which allowed them to spoil her with pampering and presents. However, Meghan and Harry wanted the world's less privileged children to also benefit from a 'baby shower' and asked fans and friends to consider making charitable donations in lieu of gifts. The result was #globalsussexbabyshower that raised large sums for a number of charities. The couple posted a message on their new Instagram account expressing their gratitude for the immense support and 'outpouring of love'.

OPPOSITE: The Duke and Duchess of Sussex introduce their newborn son to the world

It was also via Instagram that Harry and Meghan, in their thoroughly modern manner, initially broke the news that, on 6 May 2019 at 5.26am, they had become the proud parents of a baby boy. Messages of congratulations poured in and within an hour the exciting news had received more than one million 'likes'.

The child weighed 7lb 3oz (3.26kg) and was born, a little overdue, at London's Portland Hospital. A beaming Harry, in his first words to the public, spoke of his joy but also of the pride he felt for his wife and paid tribute to mothers, saying, 'what any woman does is beyond comprehension'.

The couple had made it clear that they intended to handle the news surrounding the birth their way and their determination to do what they felt was right for them was seen immediately following the event when Meghan spent a couple of days at home at Frogmore Cottage, enjoying private family time before presenting her baby to the public in a structured photoshoot. On the same day as the photoshoot, her son's names were announced: Archie Harrison Mountbatten-Windsor.

The Queen was 'delighted' at the news about her eighth great grandchild. The boy is the fourth grandchild of Prince Charles, who expressed his pleasure and commented that he was 'collecting rather a large number of them'. He is the first grandchild of Meghan's mother Doria who arrived from the US in the days prior to the birth and stayed at Frogmore Cottage.

Little Archie, seventh in line to the throne, will be raised surrounded by love and encouraged to develop values in line with those of his parents. As a nation we celebrate this child, part of a forward-thinking modern generation of a Royal Family that strives to break down cultural barriers to create a fairer, more tolerant world.

Presenting her son at St George's Hall, Windsor Castle, Meghan described him as having 'the sweetest temperament, he's really calm. He's been the dream'

A New Chapter

In the space of her first year as Duchess of Sussex, Meghan gained enormous respect and earned an enviable reputation. For her, coming from a culture more informal than the one to which her husband was born, it was a steep learning curve; she had to become acquainted with not only the customs and way of life of the Royal Family itself – not to mention its numerous members – but also with the culture of her adopted country. She had to familiarise herself with British etiquette and royal protocol, while coping with the demands of a very different working life to the one she had experience of in her previous career as an actress. Her role as Duchess is one she could never have prepared for nor envisaged for

OPPOSITE: The Duke and Duchess of Sussex were looking forward to the birth of their first child when this photograph was taken, and became proud parents in May 2019

herself when she was growing up in Los Angeles and working in the USA and Canada.

Her gentle, caring, yet highly capable and professional nature has won the hearts of the British people as well as those of her new extended family. Importantly, Meghan has brought a fresh, less formal element to the Royal Family that has its roots steeped in history, pomp and ceremony. Meghan, in conjunction with her husband and the Duke and Duchess of Cambridge, has played her part in creating a dynamic style of monarchy relevant to the 21st century and its modern mores. This is an aspect that the Duchess of Sussex will continue to develop, alongside her work for gender and racial equality – topics close to her heart that she will still be in a position to influence.

Since the birth of her son on 6 May 2019, Meghan has entered a new chapter in her life, that of a mother. Both she and Harry have, through their working lives, demonstrated a natural affinity with children and they have professed a determination to give their child as normal a life as possible, away from the public gaze, while surrounded by plenty of love and attention from them as caring, responsible parents. Furthermore, with her passion to bring about positive change in the world, particularly in terms of opportunities for young people, and just as her mother did before her, Meghan is certain to instil admirable qualities in her own offspring based on hard work, commitment and an understanding of the issues faced by those less fortunate. Prior to the birth, Meghan, speaking on International Women's Day in March, also made it clear that her child would be brought up a feminist, whether the baby was a boy or a girl; quoting a documentary she had recently seen, she said, 'I feel the embryonic kicking of feminism.'

Prince Harry, with his warm personality, candid openness and self-deprecating humour, is one of the most popular members of the Royal Family. In Meghan he found his perfect complement, the ideal partner for the 'People's Prince'. Now, as new parents, this charming royal couple can look forward to even more exciting times in the years ahead.

First published in the United Kingdom in 2019 by

Pitkin Publishing

43 Great Ormond Street

London WC1N 3HZ

An imprint of Pavilion Books Ltd

www.pavilionbooks.com

+44 (0)20 7462 1500

Written by Halima Sadat; the author has asserted her moral rights

Edited by Sophie Nickelson and Gill Knappett

Picture research by Sophie Nickelson and Gill Knappett

Layouts by Ginny Zeal

All photographs by kind permission of PA Images, except for the following:

Alamy: 8, 9, 11, 14, 17, 19, 22, 25, 35 bottom, 61, 63 bottom, 85;

Getty Images: 90.

A CIP catalogue for this book is available from the British Library

Reproduced by Rival Colour Limited, UK

Printed and bound by GPS Group P.E., Slovenia

ISBN 978-1-841658-47-6   1/19

MIX
Paper from
responsible sources
FSC® C118234
www.fsc.org